To Rory

This edition published 1989 by Guild Publishing
By arrangement with Kingfisher Books Ltd,
Elsley House, 24–30 Great Titchfield Street,
London W1P 7AD.

First published in 1989 by Kingfisher Books

CN 3969

Edited by Vanessa Clarke
Phototypeset by Rowland Phototypesetting,
Bury St Edmunds, Suffolk
Printed in Spain.

The Kingfisher
Picture
Word
Book

Jane Salt
Illustrated by
Sarah Pooley

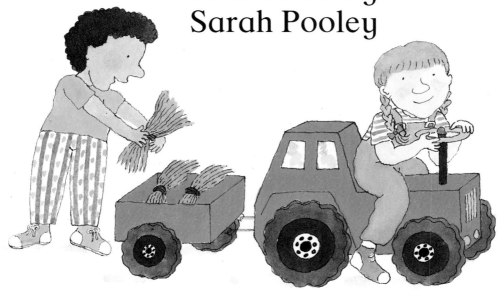

GUILD PUBLISHING
LONDON · NEW YORK · SYDNEY · TORONTO

Introduction

Here are some ways in which you can help your child enjoy and learn with this book.

● Let your child spend as long as he or she likes on each page. Some pages will be looked at enthusiastically, others will be flicked over and returned to later.

● Talking and listening are very important. Help your child's conversational skills by discussing what the characters are doing.

● Prediction skills are essential for learning to read. Help encourage this by asking questions such as "What do you think that girl will do next?"

● Introduce your child to the printed word by pointing out some of the words you know she or he is interested in. Don't try to point out all the words at one time.

● Looking carefully plays an important part in the process of learning to read. Help your child develop visual skills by pointing out small details in the pictures.

● Do give your child plenty of opportunity to browse through the book on his or her own. Private enjoyment of books is a very special and useful habit to foster.

This book is designed to be a fun way to learn. We hope you and your child will have many hours of enjoyment with it.

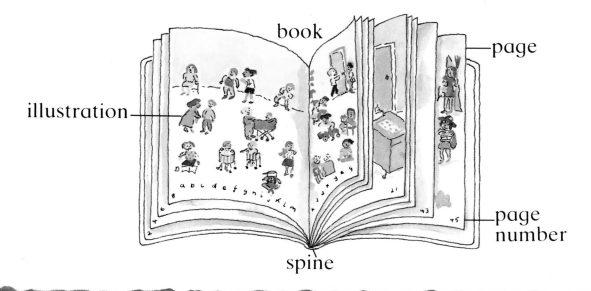

Contents

I like books!

Alphabet names

Look for the letter that begins your name.

Hussam

hiding

Gertie

giggling

Beep!

umbrella

Vicky

van

Isabelle

Whoops!

ink

Jin Hee

jeans

Leo

letter

Min Wei

mud

Katie

kitten

Yasmin

yawning

wet

Umberto

William

Max

box

Zeff

zoo

The birthday party

Happy Birthday to you!

Happy Birthday to you!

Mum

Dad

candle

Granny

Uncle

brother

cake

baby

Grandad

sister

high chair

dog

10

balloons

Grandpa

cousin

Auntie

cat

Nanna

card

present

wrapping paper

ribbon

11

Homes

A house always stays in the same place, but some homes can move about.

houseboat

mobile home/caravan

block of flats

Let's play house

tent

den

cave Hard rock cave

cottage/house

bungalow

space house

nest

castle

Where shall I put the flag?

13

The doll's house – outside . . .

When you open the front door of the doll's house, you can see all the rooms inside.

. . . and inside

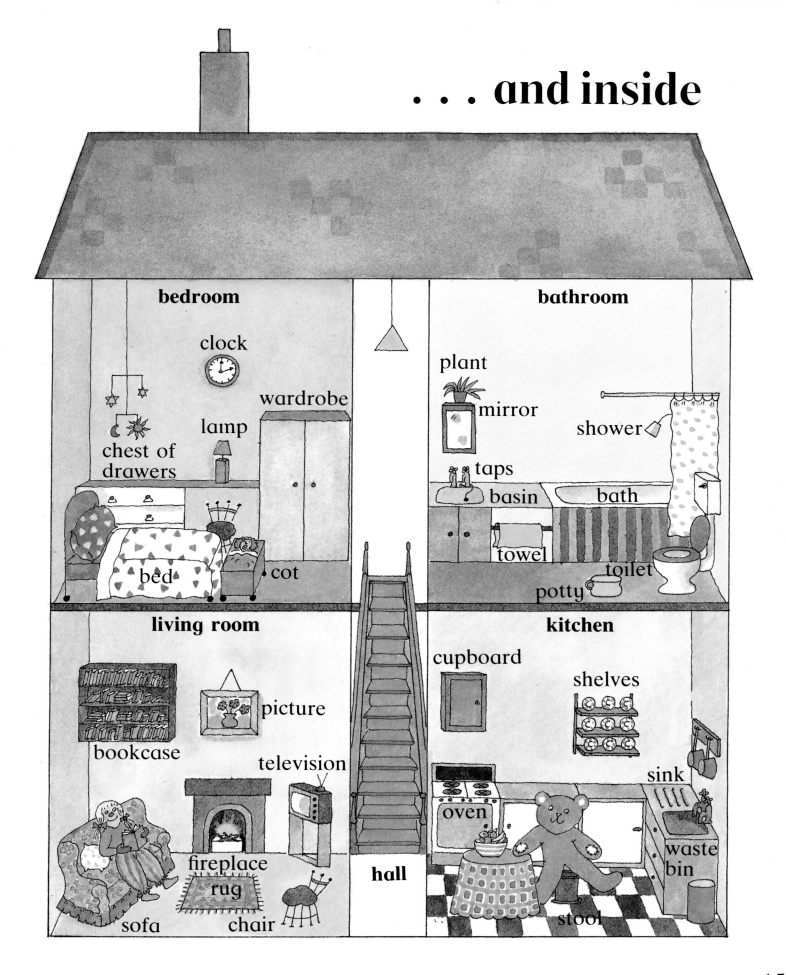

bedroom

clock

wardrobe

lamp

chest of drawers

bed

cot

bathroom

plant

mirror

shower

taps

basin

bath

towel

toilet

potty

living room

picture

bookcase

television

fireplace

rug

sofa

chair

hall

kitchen

cupboard

shelves

sink

oven

waste bin

stool

Time to eat

breakfast

dinner and lunch

Make a menu by writing down
your favourite kinds of food.

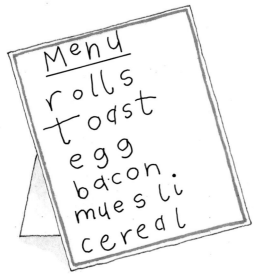

teacup

sugar

saucer

spoon

mug

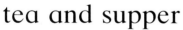

tea and supper

apron

washing-up bowl

washing-up liquid

bowl

tea-towel

washing-up

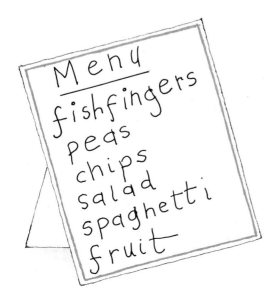

Menu
fishfingers
peas
chips
salad
spaghetti
fruit

In the city

hospital

school

Out Patients

PUDDLEDUCK HOSPITAL

HEALTH CENTRE

NOW SHOWING... "BABES-IN-THE-WOOD"

PALACE THEATRE

Starring Ivy Leaf and Lily Bud

PARK ROAD SCHOOL

sign

fire-engine

park

synagogue

PUDDLE DUCK PARK

LAUNDERETTE

pedestrian crossing

car

cinema

traffic-lights

Maps tell us how to find the streets we want.

pavement

map

18

mosque

factory

offices

church

museum

police
station

POLICE

St. Vincent's Church

library

road

lamp-post

restaurant

van

shop

Café des Amis

A spotless Wash!

Greengrocers

Daphne's
Hairdresser

POST OFFICE

bicycle

bus

street

The check-up

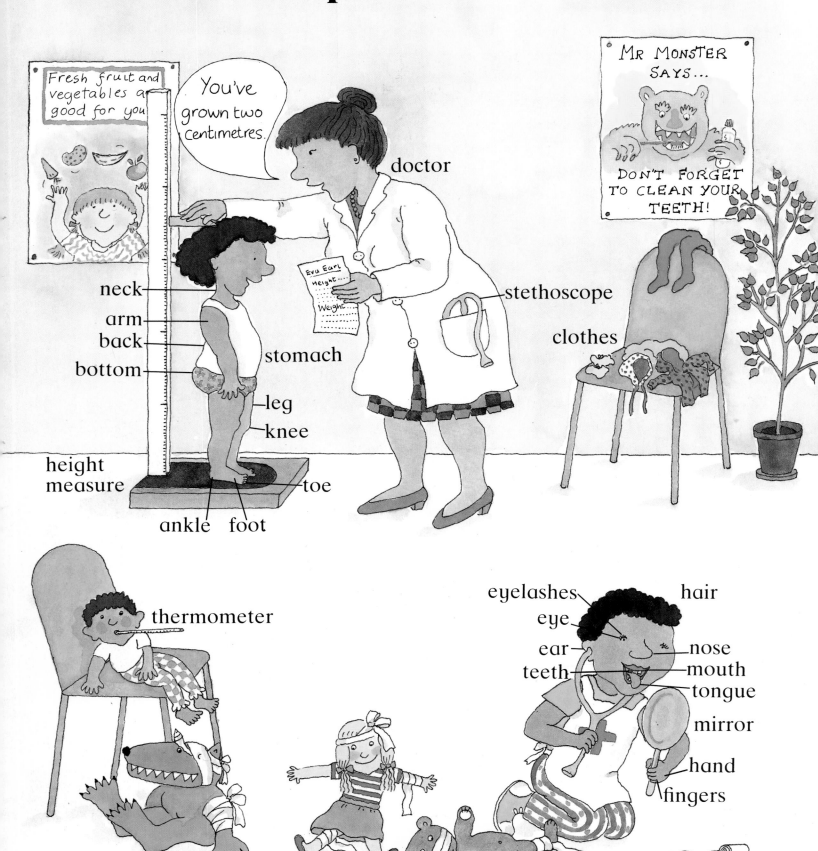

Fresh fruit and vegetables are good for you

You've grown two centimetres.

doctor

MR MONSTER SAYS... DON'T FORGET TO CLEAN YOUR TEETH!

neck
arm
back
bottom

stomach

stethoscope

clothes

leg
knee

height measure

toe

ankle   foot

thermometer

eyelashes
eye
ear
teeth

hair

nose
mouth
tongue

mirror

hand

fingers

bandage

School-days

music corner

shakers

drum

bookcase

bookcorner

parent

felt pens

crayons

funnel

bubbles

beaker

cushion

book

Higher!

jug

bricks

telephone

clothes box

teacher

apron

waste-paper basket

home corner

nature corner

table

chair

Messy!

paint

23

Clothes

wardrobe

shirt/blouse

dress

dungarees

coat

boots

sweater

trainers

vest

pants

pyjamas

slippers

trousers

dressing-gown

T-shirt

skirt

belt

tights

socks

shoes

Colours

paintbrush

white   black   red   blue   green

Dressing-up clothes

Where's that spell for turning princes into frogs?

broomstick

witch

prince

wizard

monster

mask

Eek!

wand

fairy

crown

clown

pirate

carnival queen

burglar

Look for the different colours in the picture.

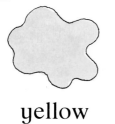

yellow

pink

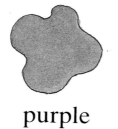

purple

orange

brown

grey

Workers

Building words

sheet

spirit-level

nails

drill

clamp

box

hammer

paint

Oops... too short!

string

plank of wood

paper

saw

scissors

work-bench

screws

screwdriver

glue

sticky cat

28

Vicky's shop

shopkeeper

customers

sign

flowerpot

29

At the supermarket

LIST
- fish fingers
- bananas
- bread
- potatoes
- milk
- yoghurt
- chicken
- cat food
- nappies
- baked beans
- orange juice

Can you help me find all these things on my shopping list?

Dairy

yoghurt

milk

cream

butter

orange juice

basket

trolley

ENTRANCE

Fruit and Vegetables

Bakery

bread

assistant

cakes

potatoes

oranges bananas

Weigh here

Groceries

baked beans

check-out till

10

10:15

chicken

receipt

money

fish fingers

Frozen foods

CHEAPIES wholewheat cereal

Food is Fresh at CHEAPIES

nappies small

nappies large

nappies medium

purse

nappies X large

nappies X large

EXIT

nappies

cat food

Food is Fresh at CHEAPIES SUPERMARKET

31

Weather words

Whether the weather be hot,
or whether the weather be not,

snowflakes
skis
snowball
sledge
icicle
ice
ice-skates
woolly hat
coat
mittens
snowman
snow
snow-shoes

snowy

hat
wind
kite
cloud
balloon
blossom
daffodils
scarf
violets
primroses

windy

We'll weather the weather,
whatever the weather,

Whether we like it or not.

T-shirt

Sausages!

barbecue

paddling
pool

roses

sun-hat

sandals

sun-dress

shorts

watering-
can

trowel

worm

sunny

lightning

C-R-A-S-H

rain

Café

cape

puddle

umbrella

drain

rainhat

rain
coat

I can
hear
thunder!

wellington boots

stormy

33

Puddleduck park

35

A picnic in the country

river

tractor

field

fence

Public footpath

Litter

Please shut the gate

Fresh fruit & veg

tree

bridge

rocks

frog

net

stream

grasshopper

dandelion

leaf

wood

hill

horses

bird's nest

picnic

Look!

binoculars

Bird guide

stepping-stones

Splash!

poppy

ants

37

yacht

windsurfer

lighthouse

cliff

beachball

snorkel

goggles

It's a sea monster!

sand-castle

spade

flippers

swimming costume

beach

sun-glasses

bucket

crab

deck-chair

rock pool

thermos

shell

hat

seaweed

book

39

Things that go

motorway
traffic jam
lorry
petrol pump
car
motorbike

petrol station

TOOTING
Platform 1
carriage
train
driver
ticket
engine
suitcase
platform

train station

racing track
engine
wheel
Whoops!
finish
start
racing car

Choo! choo!
goods train
station
signal
track
railway crossing

40

Cars, trains, boats and aeroplanes
are all different kinds of transport.

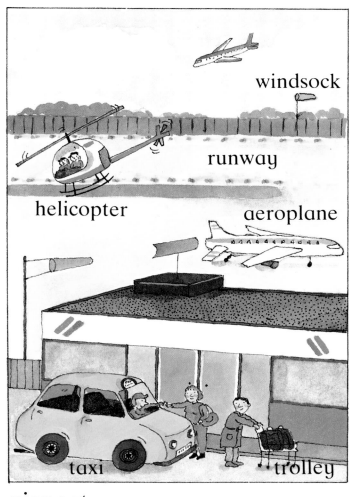

airport

harbour

glider

jet

41

Animal friends

The animals went in two by two,
The elephant and the kangaroo.

panda

kangaroos

horses

dog

lions

leopards

penguin

monkeys

seals

I can't find
the other tiger.
Can you see
it?

elephants

rabbit

squirrels

Noah's Ark

cats

snakes

tiger

ostriches

gorillas

deer

polar
bear

hippopotamus

sheep

duck

giraffe

crocodiles

foxes

43

Sizes . . .

The clown is tall,
but teddy is short.

1m
2m

How tall are you?

high
low

tall

short

large

JIGSAW

small

light

heavy

circle

square

triangle

tiny

enormous

fat

thin

little

big

. . . and shapes

Look for these shapes in the picture.

rectangle   heart   oval   star

45